Divorce &
See What's Hiding Behind My Smile

by Mason A. Marovic

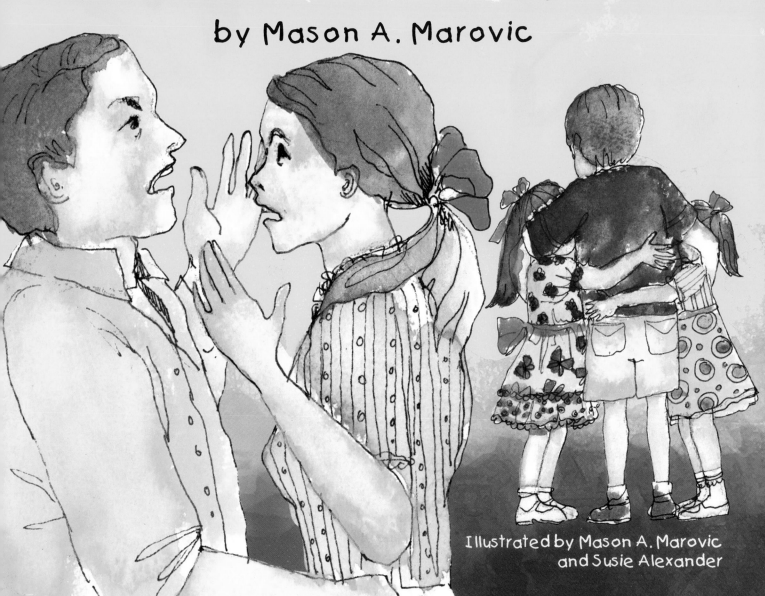

Illustrated by Mason A. Marovic
and Susie Alexander

Copyright © 2009 by Mason A. Marovic. 47375-MARO
Library of Congress Control Number: 2008911452
ISBN: Softcover 978-1-4363-9171-9
       Hardcover 978-1-4363-9172-6

This book was printed in the United States of America.

To order additional copies of this book, contact:
Xlibris Corporation
1-888-795-4274
www.Xlibris.com
Orders@Xlibris.com

Dedication

I dedicate this book to my mom. My mom is always there for me. She helps me talk about my feelings. She reads to me at night when the house is quiet and it is just the two of us.

I dedicate this book to my sisters, Samantha & Jenna. They were only 2 ½ and 3 ½ when my parents got a divorce. They had the same feelings I did, but they did not understand what was happening.

I dedicate this book to all the children of divorce. I hope it will help them talk about their feelings and let others know how they feel. I bet a lot of kids hide their feelings behind their smiles, like I do.

Thank you Susie for sketching my visions and teaching me to watercolor. I had fun learning from you and talking with you. We always had fun!

I have so many feelings, but I hide them
behind my smiling face.
Everyone can see the smile on my face,
but behind that smile is a sad face.

I feel sad because my parents are getting a divorce.

Sometimes, I feel hurt when my parents argue, but I hide my feelings behind my smile.

Sometimes, I feel sad because my daddy doesn't live with us anymore, but I hide my feelings behind my smile.

Sometimes, I feel angry because I did not have a choice about what is happening, but I hide my feelings behind my smile.

13

Sometimes, I feel scared because I think that maybe my parents are getting a divorce because of me, even though they reassure me it is only between them, but I hide my feelings behind my smile.

Sometimes, I feel worried because I am unsure of what the plans are, who will take care of me, and where I am going to spend the night, but I hide my feelings behind my smile.

Sometimes, I feel over protective because
I have 2 little sisters that are scared
and unsure too, but I hide my
feelings behind my smile.

Sometimes, I feel frustrated because I don't like all of the changes that are happening and I don't know how to express my emotions, but I hide my feelings behind my smile.

Sometimes, I feel ashamed to tell people that my parents are getting divorced, but I hide my feelings behind my smile.

Sometimes, I feel guilty telling my mom how much fun I had with my dad or telling my dad how much fun I had with my mom, but I hide my feelings behind my smile.

Sometimes, I feel disappointed because
I don't spend holidays with my mom and
dad together, but I hide my feelings
behind my smile.

My smile is big, my smile is bright, my smile is true because although I have all those feelings, what I am sure of is that my mom and dad love me no matter how I feel, what happens, or where they live.

All of my feelings, concerns,
and thoughts are mine,
but they are probably a lot
like yours.

When parents get divorced
we often hide our feelings &
emotions behind our smiles.

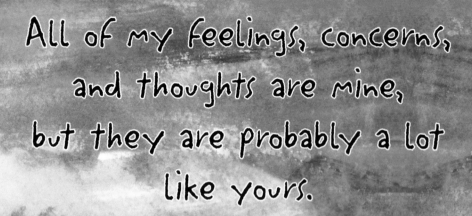

What is hiding behind your smile?

EXHAUSTED

ANGRY

ASHAMED

DEPRESSED

LONELY

ANXIOUS

SAD

BORED

CONFIDENT

ENRAGED

SURPRISED

ECSTATIC

What is hiding behind your smile?

HAPPY

FRUSTRATED

LOVESTRUCK

FRIGHTENED

SHY

HOPEFUL

OVERWHELMED

CAUTIOUS

SMUG

SUSPICIOUS

ASHAMED

CONFUSED

Directions: Fill in the blanks.
Write how you feel and when you feel like that.
Draw the face you make when you feel like that.

Sometimes I feel _____ when _____

_____

Sometimes I feel _____ when _____

_____

Sometimes I feel ＿＿＿＿＿＿＿＿when ＿＿＿＿＿＿＿

＿＿＿＿＿＿＿＿＿＿＿＿＿＿＿＿＿＿＿＿＿＿＿＿＿＿＿＿

Sometimes I feel _____ when _____

_____

Sometimes I feel _____ when _____

_____

Sometimes I feel _____ when _____

_____

Sometimes I feel _____ when _____

_____

Sometimes I feel _____ when _____

_____